Modernized Accounting & Technology for the Small Business Owner

Increase Your Profits and Productivity

Noel B. Lorenzana, CPA

Copyright © 2018 Noel B. Lorenzana

All rights reserved.

CONTENTS

1	Introduction	Pg 1
2	About the Author	Pg 3
3	The Basics	Pg 5
4	Going Paperless, Apps, and the Cloud	Pg 9
5	Automate and Innovate Your Accounting Process	Pg 18
6	Best Security Practices for Online Accounting	Pg 24
7	Gain Time and Create Leverage by Outsourcing	Pg 31
8	Accounting for Profits	Pg 36
9	Fear Not, the IRS	Pg 45
10	Your Accountant	Pg 53
11	Understanding Financial Statements	Pg 60
12	Final Thoughts	Pg 67

CHAPTER 1

INTRODUCTION

If you're like most business owners, you're always looking for ways to grow and improve your business without devoting more hours into your schedule or spending more money that may not produce results. Wouldn't it be nice to save some money and free up a few hours each week? This is where technology is available to make life easier.

Leveraging the right tools and strategies can make a massive difference in how efficiently you run your company. Tech-savvy business owners are saving money and time, while also allowing themselves more flexibility and solving problems that would have been very hard to address a decade ago. Sadly, those who

Modernized Accounting & Technology for the Small Business Owner

are hesitant to take advantage of technology will miss out and may find it difficult to compete.

The goal of this book is to show you how current technology and internet-based applications can help you grow without compromising the quality of your business. These tools can help you access a wealth of data about your business, and the ability to easily and quickly share that data with your team. You can then leverage that information into proactive decisions. If so, your overall life will improve and your business is about to take a leap forward.

CHAPTER 2

ABOUT THE AUTHOR

Before we take this journey together, here's a little bit about me. My name is Noel B. Lorenzana. I'm a Registered Certified Public Accountant, licensed in Illinois. I've spent the past 25 years in business, tax, and accounting, including over 17 years of operations, management, and accounting for a specialty food importer and distributor.

For the past several years, I've turned my attention to helping small business owners improve their profits and get better results by combining technology, strategy, and proactive accounting. As a

Modernized Accounting & Technology for the Small Business Owner

Certified Tax Resolution Specialist, I've also had the chance to represent many taxpayers and help them resolve their tax problems.

It's been a pleasure helping taxpayers and business owners get great results. Throughout this book, I hope to help you see better results too. The starting point is a fast and flexible accounting system to allow you to be proactive, rather than reactive. A system that shares information with everyone on your team, both in and out of your physical office. A system that connects your accounting to your marketing and operations, so you can fully optimize these areas and track your progress.

I'm excited to think what that progress will look like for your business. I hope you are too. Let's get started!

CHAPTER 3

THE BASICS

Whether you're just getting started in business or are an experienced business owner looking to level up your results, you will find something helpful in this book. The world we do business in differs greatly from what it was even 10 to 15 years ago. Everything moves fast, electronically, and in "the cloud." Whether you're an online business, a traditional business, or both, the internet has been a game changer in the way businesses operate. If you're not there yet, don't worry, that just means you have room to get even better results!

Modernized Accounting & Technology for the Small Business Owner

You'll find information in this book on many topics, including types of technology you can use, best practices, risks, benefits, using technology to connect with clients/employees/contractors, and how technology can benefit the relationship with one of your most important partners, your accountant.

Many ideas you can implement and immediately see a benefit. Some work better together and the more you integrate these ideas, the more momentum you'll get. Once you see results, you'll want to keep increasing that leverage. You may even get a little addicted to the time savings and efficiency of modernizing your business's accounting system. Let's talk about that system for a minute.

YOUR ACCOUNTING SYSTEM

Accountants talk about accounting differently than non-accountants. We talk about it as the language of business. Accounting is like a doctor of internal medicine, analyzing what's going on beneath the surface that may not be obvious from the outside. Large corporations have entire accounting departments providing them with real-time data and analysis whenever they must make a decision. Small and medium-sized businesses are at a big disadvantage if they can't harness accurate and up-to-date information. This is where a good accounting system comes in.

When businesses start, they often do their own books and simply hand over the information to an accountant or tax person at the end of the year to get their taxes done. This works for a while. But... there is a big gap between this start-up stage and the stage of growth where you'll bring on an in-house accountant or accounting department. This gap is where it's crucial to put systems in place and leverage technology. If you're reading this book (and you are) it's likely that your business is in this gap right now.

DECODING THE LANGUAGE OF BUSINESS

So, if accounting is the language of business and you want your business to thrive, what can you do? If you're in that gap between do-it-yourself and an in-house accountant, you can use technology in two major ways. You can use it to connect and communicate with accounting professionals. You can also use it to make better decisions by having timely, accurate information more accessible.

Maybe you're just outgrowing the do-it-yourself phase, and it's getting hard to keep up with your accounting. Technology and modern accounting workflows can make it easier and allow you to do the job better. The right tools and strategies can help you get by on your own longer and make a smoother transition to working with professionals as your business grows.

If you're further along but not ready for your own accountant just yet, you can leverage technology to create a virtual accounting team who can work together without the expense of office space or

Modernized Accounting & Technology for the Small Business Owner

having your own accountant on staff. Now you're connected to experts who can guide you through fast, complex conversations and help you get to where you want to go.

Wherever you are on the journey, I'm excited that you're considering trying to use modernized accounting in your business. I'm also excited that I get to be a part of your growth. With no more delay, let's jump into it and talk about tech-savvy business strategies and why you should consider adopting technology if you haven't already.

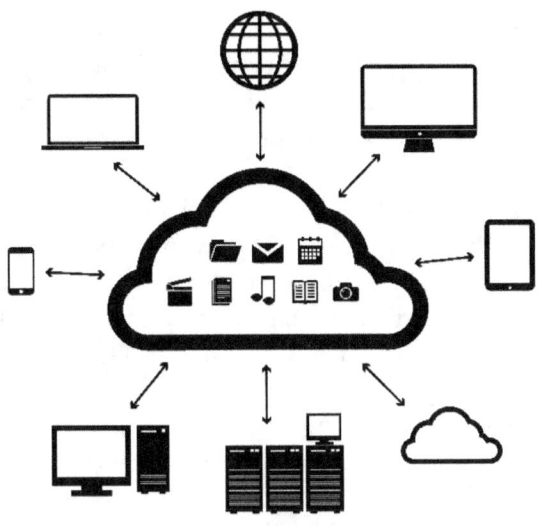

CHAPTER 4

GOING PAPERLESS, APPS, AND THE CLOUD

Some accountants are on the old-fashioned side. Maybe that's you. You like to follow a traditional approach and do the things that have always worked. Why change something that's working well? However, there's a catch.

There are two kinds of change: the kind we make ourselves and the kind beyond our control. We can decide not to change, but our surroundings will always change and move around us. Before we get

Modernized Accounting & Technology for the Small Business Owner

too deep and philosophical, here's the point. The change will happen whether we like it or not because it is beyond our control and affects how we relate to our world even if we remain static.

Today's business world is changing faster than ever, and if we don't keep up, we will be left behind. Every day more businesses we serve will utilize technology, and they expect the same speed and efficiencies from their accountants. Like an older computer trying to run new programs, some traditional accounting office practices aren't compatible with the changing landscape.

If you're not already tech-savvy, stepping up in this area will bring a big boost to your accounting process and your business. If you are, you may need to brush up on the tools and strategies to bring that tech into your accounting process. In broad strokes, there are a few major areas where technology allows us to handle bookkeeping and accounting tasks more efficiently.

GOING PAPERLESS

Saving trees and reducing waste is always a good thing, but there is much more to a paperless office than environmental benefits. Cost is one of the obvious benefits. Keeping files digitized, rather than on paper, saves not only on paper costs and ink but also the space and cost of storing all those paper files and shredding them for security when they're no longer needed.

Increase Your Profits and Productivity
Noel B. Lorenzana, CPA

Digital files are also much faster to find and can be accessed by several people at once from different locations. You can also access files from outside the office, which can save you trips to the office to look something up or even enable you to work from home or just about anywhere. You determine who has access and who doesn't. There is a brief learning curve while you learn and create the system, but it will save you so much time retrieving files!

APPS

Gone are the days when apps were just games for people to play on their smartphones. There are hundreds of apps available for businesses, and they can save you both time and manual data entry. Many apps sync automatically with the accounting software available (which we will talk about later) and can update information with the touch of a button.

Check the website for your accounting software to get ideas for great apps you can use. There are likely several that would help your business track time, communicate, keep receipts and other documents in order, etc. I would recommend you start with one at a time, progressing slowly, before adding another. Shiny object syndrome can make it tempting to use several new apps at once, but you won't get the best results from any of them if you don't learn to use them well.

Here are just a few ways you can use apps to modernize and simplify your accounting:

Modernized Accounting & Technology for the Small Business Owner

TIME TRACKING

If you have hourly employees or independent contractors, for whom you must track time for, there's an app for that. You can track everything by employee name and also track which projects they were working on during various times.

This not only gives you the hours for preparing payroll, but it also helps you track billable hours or figure out how much time was spent on a fixed-rate project for a client. You may discover you've been undercharging for your services or that a certain employee or contractor is taking too long on a job. TSheets is one of the most popular apps for this and may even come included with your version of QuickBooks Online if that's the software you're using.

RECEIPT TRACKING

Keeping track of your receipts without filling a drawer or the proverbial shoebox is a big step toward modernizing your accounting. Trust me, and your tax preparer will thank you. There are several applications to help you organize receipts. Essentially, you take a digital picture or scan of a document and save that instead of the physical paper.

I'm sure you can see the benefits of not holding onto paper receipts and trying to find them later. Besides the mess and time you save, you also have permanent documents. If you buy anything for your business from a retailer who uses tape receipts, the ink fades and eventually becomes unreadable. If you make online purchases, you likely get emailed receipts anyway. Now you can save them in the same app rather than printing off paper copies of your paperless digital receipts.

Now for the best part. Your receipts can be attached to transactions in your accounting software, so you have instant access to the verifying document when you're looking at a purchase or expense. All that detail is right at your fingertips!

MILEAGE TRACKING

Mileage can be a great deduction for your business. If you travel to job sites or client meetings, go to the client's home or place of business to serve them, or run out to pick up supplies or ship something out, you could deduct all that mileage on your taxes. However, how do you track and verify that mileage? Let an app like MileIQ do it for you.

Unlike some other apps I've mentioned, which run on your computer, you'll have a mileage tracking app that will work on your phone. When you commute for business, the GPS in your phone tracks the miles and logs them as either business or personal. You can sync this mileage with your accounting software and keep a running total.

Modernized Accounting & Technology for the Small Business Owner

Digital Signatures

Now that you're going paperless and keeping files in digital formats, wouldn't it be great if you could get signatures on client contracts and paperwork without printing and faxing? Faxing feels like a carryover from a different era, and in many offices, it only sticks around because of the need to sign agreements.

There are great tools to handle this, with DocuSign being one of the most popular. You can get different features and price points in these apps depending on what you need and how often you need to use it. You'll use a touchscreen on your smartphone or laptop mouse to sign your name and apply it to the document. The app can track progress and update both parties when the intended person signs, sending a final copy to both, by email.

A digital signature carries the same legal weight as a physical signature, in almost all cases, so it makes sense for most people to make the change. This is especially true if you serve clients remotely and don't meet with them in person. You'll save time onboarding new clients and can get rid of that extra phone line and that bulky, noisy fax machine in the corner of your office. If you still need fax capabilities, there are inexpensive online options like eFax that allows you to fax documents just like having a traditional fax machine without the additional phone line.

Increase Your Profits and Productivity
Noel B. Lorenzana, CPA

If running these apps sounds like juggling fire, no worries. One of the easiest ways to wrangle them all at once is to start with your accounting software and use it as a platform to connect all your other applications.

ACCOUNTING SOFTWARE

I've mentioned accounting software several times already. Whether you're handling the bookkeeping and accounting in-house or having it done by a remote professional, you'll need an accounting software package to coordinate it all. The software allows access for a remote bookkeeper or accountant without the need for someone to come to your office or use additional fancy software hacks to access your computer remotely.

QuickBooks has been the most popular small business accounting software in the United States for many years. QuickBooks Online is the cloud-based version. This means you aren't forced to install it on a certain computer; it resides on the internet, and you can access it with your account from anywhere. It also means it is always updated and current, with no need to buy a new version every few years. Xero is another accounting software option gaining popularity with the small business owner. It was designed with cloud computing as it's core and focuses on intuitive design for enhanced user experience.

Once you've found the best fit for you, look at the applications compatible with your software.

Modernized Accounting & Technology for the Small Business Owner

QuickBooks Online, for example, has an ecosystem of hundreds of applications that will sync with QuickBooks Online including the apps mentioned earlier. This lets you easily move items from one app to another and keeps everything organized.

Remember the Password

We'll go into more depth on security later, but for now, let's discuss passwords and accessing these apps. Once you get a few applications up and running, it may feel like you have too many logins and passwords to keep track of. Many still use post-it notes on their computer monitor to save the information, but there are better options.

LastPass is a popular option for keeping all of your login data accessible and secure. You can enter usernames and passwords for many applications and websites and access them with the click of a button from within LastPass. All you have to do is enter one password to log in to LastPass, and you'll be able to open all of your apps from there. You can also grant access to other people who need to access your apps or software without actually giving them the passwords. That way, you can remove their access when the job is finished.

Get Your Head in the Cloud

By now, you're probably familiar with cloud computing, but then again you may not be. If not, let's talk about it for a minute. In the past, we stored

Increase Your Profits and Productivity
Noel B. Lorenzana, CPA

all of our computer data on our individual computers. If I stored files about clients, I had them saved on a hard drive in my office and backed them up somewhere off-site in case something happened to my computer.

With cloud computing or "the cloud", information is stored remotely rather than on your computer. It's not much different from the way Google stores your email. You can log in to your account and access your emails, but they aren't saved and stored on your computer. Now you can do the same thing with all kinds of information and software.

Because it isn't on your office computer, you can access it from anywhere. There are security measures in place to prevent unauthorized access, and the fact that it is continuously backed up off-site prevents you from losing valuable information if you have an office fire, a break-in, or if your hardware crashes.

There are security risks with cloud computing. But, traditional data storage systems come with risks as well. Small businesses often do not have the budget for implementing security systems and maintaining security technology. The cloud service company provides the hardware and current security measures. Implementing a new system comes with risks to consider, but it's also clear that the benefits of cloud computing can be a factor to help your business grow.

CHAPTER 5

AUTOMATE AND INNOVATE YOUR ACCOUNTING PROCESS

So far, we've looked at various tech tools and how they can help you. Putting a few tools together can allow you to achieve the holy grail of business tech, computer automation. Let's look at some processes you can automate in your business to cut down on manual entry and save you a bunch of time.

For this chapter, let's use QuickBooks Online as an example so that we have one streamlined workflow to look at. You can do something very similar in most other full cloud accounting programs, so unless you're using a lighter software application like Wave or FreshBooks, this applies to you.

AUTOMATE YOUR EXPENSES

One of the accounting tasks that small businesses deal with daily is entering and classifying transactions. Some put it off until the end of the month and do it all at once, which makes for one dreaded day. Others hand this day to day task off to a bookkeeper as soon as possible. For some, that means bringing in a professional, but others just add another job to the receptionist's duties and call them an administrative assistant instead.

This is a bad idea if that person doesn't understand bookkeeping or the inner workings of your business. It will either result in you answering more questions than if you did it yourself or wishing the bookkeeper had asked more questions when you discover the things they assumed to be correct were not.

If you have no professional handling your books yet, it's best to be personally involved, so you know what's happening with your finances. One way to make this more feasible for the busy business owner is to automate the process as much as possible, so you only have to review and approve it.

In QuickBooks Online (QBO), you start the automation process by connecting your bank and credit cards to your QBO account. If you haven't already done this, you can go into the "banking" section on the left side menu and find options to connect your bank. This is a secure connection between your bank and QuickBooks, and only grants read only access. Once your bank is connected, you can update your bank feeds with one click and get up-to-date transactions for each linked account.

Syncing your bank accounts to QuickBooks Online is a great way to automate the process because you'll be eliminating almost all manual data entry. Now, you simply classify each transaction and put it in its proper place. QuickBooks will attempt to guess at the categories but be careful with any transaction that isn't consistent. If you've never used a particular vendor before, or if you've bought a variety of items from the same vendor, QuickBooks' auto filling may not be correct.

Do you want to take your bank feed automation up a notch? Find the "bank rules" button at the top of the bank feed screen. When you set up a bank rule, it tells QuickBooks how to classify a transaction based on certain criteria. You can set all transactions from a vendor to a certain account, or you can sort them by dollar amount. For instance, all expenses over $100 can be set to classify one way, and all under $100 can be classified another way. Pay attention to how your bank labels each transaction. Bank rules will match information from the bank details line, which often uses abbreviations of company names.

Increase Your Profits and Productivity
Noel B. Lorenzana, CPA

Bank rules can be set to add transactions automatically or to auto-fill the information so you can review and click "add" to each one. Auto adding takes automation a step further and saves you time, but be careful. If you don't always classify a particular vendor, in the same way, you'll want a chance to review those items before they go into your accounting register.

An excellent example of where auto adding is helpful is with a vendor you always use for one item. For instance, if you pay $29 every month for a specific item or service, you can be confident that a bank rule for that vendor's bank detail description and "$29" will be correct. In this example, the transaction would go straight from the bank feed to your books without even needing you to review and approve.

AUTOMATE YOUR INVOICING

Invoicing is another area that can be time-consuming. Depending on what you sell, you may automate this process and make it much more straightforward.

The simplest invoicing is recurring clients who pay the same amount each month. For instance, with clients who pay a fixed monthly fee for a service that doesn't change from month to month. You can create a recurring invoice in QuickBooks Online for a client like this, and it will be automatically emailed to the client on the days you specify. You can do the same

Modernized Accounting & Technology for the Small Business Owner

with a recurring sales receipt, so the payment method on file is charged, and the receipt is sent by email, without the client having to do anything on their end. Importantly, make sure you have their permission on file to charge their account on an ongoing basis.

What if your invoices aren't so consistent? If you have clients whose invoices change from month to month but are still similar (for instance, someone who buys one product from you in different volumes each month) you can do the same recurring invoice as above but select a "reminder" instead of sending it out automatically. This frees from having to remember and then create the invoice while still giving you a chance to review and adjust the invoice each month before sending it.

AUTOMATE YOUR BILLS

Sure, you have bills you pay for on occasion, but there are usually several regular bills you must take care of for your business. What if you could make that process quicker and sync those bills to your bookkeeping software simultaneously? That's a win.

If you're using QuickBooks Online, you have a few options. First, they offer an option called Bill Pay for QuickBooks which is useful for many small businesses. It automates the bill payment process and gives you more control and insight. It allows you to pay your bills from within QBO and automatically records the payments in the accounting ledger. You have more options with Bill Pay than you would with

Increase Your Profits and Productivity
Noel B. Lorenzana, CPA

paying bills through your bank, including the auto entry mentioned and the ability to track when things are finalized.

Bill.com is a step up from Bill Pay because it has more options and more robust features around approving payments. As your business grows and requires multiple people to approve a payment, Bill.com offers that functionality. You can select different people in your office, or even your accountant, and decide who must approve or review a payment before sending it out.

Bill.com also offers the option of having checks printed and mailed for a small fee; this is helpful if you have vendors who don't accept electronic payments yet.

CHAPTER 6

BEST SECURITY PRACTICES FOR ONLINE ACCOUNTING

One of the biggest concerns about online accounting for many business owners is security. They worry that having all that sensitive information online would be a risk and that they are putting themselves in danger of getting hacked.

Cloud-based accounting software, along with the reputable apps that connect to it, is comparatively safe. We've all been using cloud-based applications for years, in an email account. Rather than your data being stored on your hard drive in your physical location, it's stored on an off-site server, which you can access from your computer anywhere.

Increase Your Profits and Productivity
Noel B. Lorenzana, CPA

The security of the servers that store your data is high. Both physical security (access to the servers and protection against hardware failure) and electronic security are a high priority for companies like Intuit and Xero. Their reputation depends on it! It's far more secure in their servers than it would be on your personal computer, or in paper form in a drawer. Many threats to your data exist, and we often get lax on taking measures to keep it safe.

How often do you backup your files? Do you have backups off-site in case of fire, flood, theft or internal malicious damage? Do you limit access to those who need it? What about all that paper? Is it locked in a fireproof, waterproof cabinet?

As you can see, keeping all your data on site isn't the safer option. Keeping it on the server of your accounting software company is like hiring a professional security team for your data. They protect it with some very intense security measures, and it is continuously backed up if anything should go wrong. And don't worry, when your data travels, the security team goes along for the ride.

Since your data is in the cloud, it must travel through the internet for you to access it. You upload new information to the cloud and download the information as you view it. They do all this with secure data encryption. Basically, the data is encrypted before transmission, then decrypted when you receive the data. This means that any data that could be intercepted along the way would remain secure because it would be unreadable. This is the same level of security used by banks when transferring sensitive information.

So, now we've discussed the basic safety of your online information, is there anything that you can do to maximize it? Essentially, the weak point in your data's security is access to the information on your end. Here are steps you can take to make sure you are safe with the way you access your online data.

DATA SECURITY

There are steps you can take to protect your business and your data. Learn to recognize phishing emails, especially those pretending to be from your bank, software provider or cloud storage provider. Never open a link or any attachment from a suspicious email. If you are uncertain, hover over the link (do not click) to examine the destination address. Install anti-malware/anti-virus security software on all devices (laptops, desktops, routers, tablets and phones) and keep software set to automatically update.

PASSWORD PROTECTION

You're already familiar with passwords, but there are things you can do to make them more secure. First, your password should be complex and difficult to guess. Various pieces of software will have requirements to make your passwords complex (such as including numbers and special characters and having a minimum length). However, you can take these measures with every password you create, whether compulsory or not.

Passwords are only as secure as they are secret. Never write down a password or keep it in an unsecured file marked "passwords." What about sharing access with someone temporarily? There's a tool for that. You may recall LastPass being mentioned earlier. This software allows you to give access to a password secured program without actually giving out the password. As soon as access is no longer needed, you can remove the shared access. This keeps you from being at the mercy of the person on the other end and his or her security measures or lack thereof.

Internal Controls

Accountants and auditors love to talk about internal controls. They are basically just a set of standards and procedures you put in place to protect the integrity of your financial information and protect yourself from employee misdeeds. If you have one or more employees, even people you trust, it's best to have controls in place for security reasons. If nothing else, it protects them from blame if something questionable should happen.

Limiting access is the simplest form of internal controls. If someone on the team doesn't need access to specific programs or files, don't give that person access or a password. This way, you know exactly

Modernized Accounting & Technology for the Small Business Owner

who has access to what. There are likely many programs you only need to access yourself.

Separation of duties is another important internal control. This means that no one should have access and authority over multiple jobs that would allow them to misuse his or her access and then cover up for themselves. For example, the person responsible for preparing checks shouldn't also approve payments and invoices.

If you manage payments with a program like Bill.com, you can set up different approvers. You can also retain the authority to approve final payments after someone else has created them. This is like the requirement of multiple signatures on checks in larger companies.

Limited Access

Sometimes, you may need to grant program access to multiple people. Your bookkeeper might need bank access to get a statement for reconciliation. Contractors or team members may need to add their hours to your time tracking software, etc. One safety measure in these situations is to grant limited access.

Most bank accounts, for example, can grant read-only access, allowing statements to be viewed but not allowing any other banking actions to be taken. Time tracking software like TSheets will enable users to enter their time, but not edit or change anything else. These forms of limited access allow flexibility without

Increase Your Profits and Productivity
Noel B. Lorenzana, CPA

compromising your data.

EXTERNAL ACCESS

With all the safety measures in place, one of the few security problems you may still be concerned about is your accounting professional. This person will need access to a large amount of information and can make changes.

The best advice I can give you is to take your time and make a wise choice. Seek a professional who understands your needs. Positive testimonials or a referral from someone you know and trust can be great, but you don't always have that luxury. Experience and credentials are other good indicators of a trustworthy professional. Most CPAs and accountants have invested in their profession, which makes it unlikely for them to risk their reputation by abusing their clients' trust.

One thing often overlooked is finding an accountant with whom you enjoy working with. Someone who takes time to explain things you may not understand and someone who is relatable. This will make it easier for you to communicate about your business needs. Staying with an accounting professional for the long term is one of the best ways to ensure that you have someone you can trust.

Another thing that a professional brings to the table is an eye for something that's not right. When your books and finances are being reviewed by an

Modernized Accounting & Technology for the Small Business Owner

experienced accountant, mistakes or questionable employee practices will often be detected and brought to your attention. You may miss these on your own, but a professional knows what your books should look like and will notice when something is wrong. Like the accounting software itself, a good outside accountant will make your operations more secure.

With a few simple measures on your end and the power of your software's security protocols, accounting technology can be both more convenient and more secure than doing things the old way.

CHAPTER 7

GAIN TIME AND CREATE LEVERAGE BY OUTSOURCING

The apps and tech tools we've been talking about can save you a ton of time and effort in running your business. They make many processes easier, but one of the most powerful things tech tools can do is enable you to delegate to people outside your organization. Cloud-based business tools allow people to work for your business, without actually being inside or even near your business. This is a game changer when you're ready to create leverage and take your business to a new level.

The term "outsourcing" has negative connotations, so let's discuss that first. Most of the negativity comes from the idea that outsourcing is taking advantage of quick, overseas, cheap labor to get things done, at the expense of quality. However, this need not be the case.

Outsourcing is merely taking a project (one time or ongoing) and having it completed by someone from outside of the company. It's a great strategy as a small business owner because you have limited staff. And, hiring new employees is expensive and time-consuming. You may also not have space for more employees.

Outsourcing isn't about hiring cheap help. Done right, it's about saving time, money and stress by hiring specialists. For example, if you must create a better web presence for your business by keeping your website and social media accounts updated, you could do that yourself, or you could outsource to an individual or company who specializes in that type of work. A specialist will be more efficient and won't have to deal with the learning curve or keeping up with the changes in technology (they keep up with changes, but you don't necessarily pay them for that). Ideally, the money you spend will be more than offset by the value created with your newly liberated time. You can now focus on what you do best.

While outsourcing on a global scale may be a complex issue for many companies, outsourcing for your business creates excellent opportunities. The use of contractors can be a great tax savings strategy; also, doing so allows you to bring in help as needed rather

Increase Your Profits and Productivity
Noel B. Lorenzana, CPA

than hiring new staff and either laying them off or paying them between projects when they aren't adding any value.

What does all this have to do with technology and your business' accounting system? There are great ways technology can enable you to connect with service providers to make outsourcing easier. We will talk about two critical members of your team (your bookkeeper and accountant) in a later chapter. So, for now, let's talk about how technology can help you work with others seamlessly.

The tech tools we talked about earlier will come in very handy when you outsource projects to contractors. Time tracking software like TSheets is helpful for tracking time spent on a project. You can grant limited access to a contractor allowing them to record their time on a job, but not edit or create manual entries. You can then import these hours into QuickBooks for payment purposes, keeping things simple.

Communication apps like Slack are also great for outsourcing. You can create a Slack channel for each project and invite only the people working on it. That means that a contractor only sees information available to him or her and you can continue to discuss proprietary company information with employees in other channels. If you accidentally send a message to the wrong person, it can be easily corrected. This is a great way to communicate about outsourced tasks without having to track emails that

Modernized Accounting & Technology
for the Small Business Owner

can easily get lost or overlooked. The entire conversation is shared in one steady flow that resembles a social media feed.

You can also use project management tools like Asana or Trello to track the progress of your outsourcing and make sure everything is on schedule. These apps allow you to delegate tasks (or portions of tasks) to multiple people, who can move them through various stages and leave comments or make notes as they go. Both apps can also attach emails and files to projects, so they are easily accessible to those responsible for handling the project.

The key to outsourcing is delegating the tasks, so you don't have to monitor and micromanage them closely. If you spend as much time coordinating the outsourced work as you would have spent doing it yourself, then you've received no benefit from outsourcing. These tools can help make the process easier, by coordinating everyone involved and making tracking simple.

Isn't there additional accounting work needed with independent contractors? Yes, and your accounting software can make keeping track of freelancers and contractors easier.

If there's a chance, you'll pay a contractor more than $600 in the tax year for services (not products) you must send them a form, a 1099-Misc, for tax reporting. Tracking these payments is made easy with your software because you can enter your contractors'

Increase Your Profits and Productivity
Noel B. Lorenzana, CPA

tax information and keep a running total of what you've paid them. With your online accounting program, you can generate the forms and have all your numbers in one convenient place when the time comes.

Talk to your tax advisor about who must receive this form beforehand. The rules generally apply to services, but there are exceptions. The IRS tax code is complex and constantly changing. By correctly setting up your accounting system, you'll be able to track payments to vendors.

Paying contractors is also easier with technology. Unlike employees who receive checks or are set up for direct deposit, your outsourced work is likely to be sporadic and require different payments to different people from month to month. Manually writing checks is time-consuming. Why not automate the process?

By transferring the hours from TSheets into your Bill.com account and then processing the payments from there can save much time. You can set up electronic payments for recurring vendors, or you can have Bill.com prepare a paper check and mail it to one-time contractors.

These tech tools will make it faster and easier to outsource work, freeing up time for you to focus on what you do best, running your company.

CHAPTER 8

ACCOUNTING FOR PROFITS

There are three areas of business vital to its success. Sales and Marketing is generating sales and new business leads. Production/Business Operations is the technical side of what happens within the business. The roles of Accounting and Taxes include gathering and recording financial transactions, tax compliance, and reporting.

Performing poorly in any of these areas can be detrimental to your business; They depend on each other. For example, if you're great at bringing in new clients and developing client relationships, but you aren't able to deliver your product in time or with consistent quality, you'll struggle to retain those clients for long.

Increase Your Profits and Productivity
Noel B. Lorenzana, CPA

If you do a great job of delivering your services but aren't marketing your business, you'll have trouble replacing the clients who turnover, and you'll lose new business to competitors who provide a lower level of service but do a better job of promoting themselves. Failing to track your finances properly can cause many problems including an unprofitable business, tax problems, and overpaying your taxes. Examples are given in Chapter 11.

In my experience, most businesses do well in one area, okay in another and poorly in the other category. By performing well in all areas, you can best position your company for success. By using the technologies discussed earlier, improvements can be made in all three areas.

Most business books focus either on increasing sales or on business operations. By focusing on Accounting, a business owner can make better business decisions. They can also have better control of their cash, increase profits and save on taxes. Accounting is often defined as the language of business. If you look at the big picture, accounting has the potential to increase your profits across the board. Let's take the next few pages to discuss how your accounting system can help you improve your marketing, sales, and operations results.

MARKETING

Although people often use the terms interchangeably, there's a subtle difference between marketing and sales. Marketing includes all the research that goes into understanding your clients and developing a product that they'll want to buy. Marketing brings customers to your business and concludes with a sale. It's more than just advertising, although that is a part of the marketing process.

One of the most significant ways your accounting system can help supercharge your marketing efforts is by providing real data on the profitability of each product line or service. Whether you're reviewing existing products or considering starting a new offering, you must know how much profit you'll generate from each sale.

Businesses often skip this step and assume that they will make money if they sell enough products or services. The fact is, most companies are making most of their money from a few products, breaking even on some, and losing money on others. The successful ones subsidize the failures, and this prevents the losers from ever being re-evaluated.

Businesses who carefully examine the profitability of each product or service can save themselves a ton of trouble and expense. For example, re-examining new products and services that aren't profitable and eliminating poorly performing ones frees up time to focus on the most profitable ones. That means more money for your business from the same investment of time and effort. Who doesn't want that?

Increase Your Profits and Productivity
Noel B. Lorenzana, CPA

Accounting can also help you determine your best clients. Some will be consistently buying the high-margin products and others will always choose the low-margin products and provide little profit. When you know which clients are the most profitable, you can take measures to market to more people like them and offer new products and services that will increase the lifetime value of your best customers.

SALES

To make profitable sales, you must know how much you're spending to advertise and close each sale. Your accounting system can provide this information. Which advertising channels are giving you the best return on your investment? Too many business owners can't answer this question. Once you can, you can focus your budget on the most profitable channels and get the best results from your money.

Are certain salespeople more profitable? Do they sell the high-margin products, while others sell the easy-to-sell, low-profit-margin products? Do certain methods of compensating your salespeople generate better returns? You can leverage your accounting data to find answers to all these questions and create a sales system that outperforms anything you've done. The alternative is pouring more money into advertising and sales without knowing what return to expect.

Modernized Accounting & Technology for the Small Business Owner

OPERATING EXPENSES

Understanding your operating expenses is foundational for most manufacturing business, but smaller companies don't always have a good system in place. Knowing how much you spend on each product you sell is crucial for decision making, pricing, and understanding how much margin you have to work with for selling expenses and taxes. If you don't have an accounting system tracking costs, you should implement one. If you're a retailer rather than a manufacturer, your system will be much simpler but still necessary.

What if you provide services instead of products? Understanding your costs in time and labor is equally critical. If you pay employees by the hour, you must know the most efficient use of employees' time and the services that are most profitable. Many businesses will find they offer services that aren't profitable. Why not eliminate those and focus on the more profitable ones? Maybe the price must be raised on these services, or if that's not possible, it may need to be eliminated if clients aren't willing to pay the higher price that costs dictate.

Often, businesses that charge a flat rate instead of hourly fail to keep a close track of the hours spent on a project. That means they have no solid link between what they are charging and what they are paying to deliver the services. Failure to track these expenses can lead to losing money on labor that isn't profitable.

Increase Your Profits and Productivity
Noel B. Lorenzana, CPA

What about those who provide services and do the work themselves rather than paying employees? Tracking how much time you spend on different services or for different clients can be very revealing. You're likely to find that some of your offerings are bringing in far more money for each hour of effort. You may not bill by the hour, but we are all being compensated for our time, whether or not we measure it that way.

What's the real benefit of all this tracking? While many business owners are trying to squeeze in a few more sales and increase their income, the savvy entrepreneur can focus on the most profitable clients, products, and services and see a huge increase in the profit that follows, using the exact same amount of time and effort that they're already using.

OUTSOURCING BY THE NUMBERS

If you're like most entrepreneurs, you started your business because you have a skill and passion and you wanted to be your own boss. The accounting, sales, and marketing of your skill may all be outside of your comfort area. It's likely that you'd be better off outsourcing these tasks, as we talked about in an earlier chapter. So, how do you use this accounting information to work with outsourced professionals?

The marketing industry is very numbers-driven and smart marketers focus on metrics. If you bring in a marketing firm to research, generate leads, or run a full advertising campaign for you, they should be willing and able to provide you with data on how much you're paying for each lead, each conversion, each sale, etc. This data is priceless when you factor it into what you know about the costs and margins of your products. All these numbers either leave you with room to profit or they don't. If they don't, a change is in order.

You may reach a point where you outsource a portion of your operations, but for most small businesses the day to day operating is what they do best and the last thing on the list they'd think to outsource. One option is to work with a cost accountant or systems expert who can help you streamline processes and become more efficient. This person should understand your industry. Ensure they have a proven record of getting results for businesses like yours by asking for references in advance.

You'll get the most out of working with a cost accountant or systems expert if you know where your inefficiencies are, based on the numbers we've been talking about. When they see where you're losing money, they can put focused effort toward plugging the leaks and optimizing your business.

Accounting and Taxes

Accounting is a common theme throughout this book. It's often been called the language of business because it breaks down the inner workings of a company into objective numbers we can analyze and understand. Unfortunately, when many business owners think about accounting and taxes, they don't think in these terms.

They think of it as a once a year (or quarter or month) necessary evil to stay in compliance with the regulatory agencies. They think about getting the bookkeeping done and tax returns, instead of seeing the opportunity to make strategic, proactive decisions that improve how the business performs and how well it generates a profit.

We've discussed ways accounting information can improve marketing, sales, and operations performance. One of the biggest pieces remaining is building a proactive strategy to minimize taxes each year. I'm not talking about tax evasion here; I'm talking about tax planning. The Internal Revenue Code is long and complex, and every taxpayer may structure his or her affairs in a way to pay no more in taxes than legally owed and to align their efforts, so it results in the most after-tax profits.

The goal is to keep the most of your money, not just reduce your tax payment. The best way to do this is to understand the tax implications of every major decision you make and allow it to help guide your choices.

One way the tools we're talking about can serve you in your tax planning is by making it easier to track and categorize expenses. Most business expenses are tax deductible but getting a handle on how they impact your bottom line requires you to know how

Modernized Accounting & Technology for the Small Business Owner

much is spent and on what. Don't be like some business owners who equate "tax deductible" with "free." Be the savvy business owner who understands the implications, thinks of expenses and income in after-tax terms, and weighs the decisions accordingly.

CHAPTER 9

FEAR NOT, THE IRS

Internal Revenue Service (IRS) is the big bad wolf of the business world. Receiving a notice of an audit can cost you thousands of dollars to have a licensed tax professional defend you in an audit. If you follow simple guidelines, you won't have to ever worry about an IRS audit.

THE AUDIT PROCESS

The IRS selects returns to audit based on many factors. They have computer programs measuring the statistical likelihood that your return is inaccurate and comparing your return to other sources of information. Even if audits seem somewhat random,

Modernized Accounting & Technology for the Small Business Owner

it's based on factors that make your return appear high-risk.

If you're selected for an audit, you'll receive a letter in your mailbox. Your heart will race as you break out in a panic. You might wonder why you received the letter in the first place even if you had your return prepared by a professional. The truth is anyone is subject to the scrutiny of the IRS for many reasons. If you receive a letter like this, seek professional help, and it's never a good idea to work with the IRS without representation. Even better, make sure you have an audit protection plan in place beforehand, so you're covered if you are ever audited (more on this later).

If you're selected for an audit, the IRS may do one of three things:

1. A correspondence audit, which takes place by mail and usually involves sending in additional documents.

2. An office audit, which requires you or your representative to come to an IRS office in person.

3. A field audit, which involves an IRS agent coming to your home, your business, or your representative's office.

Wherever the audit takes place, the agents involved are there to maximize their tax revenue and

Increase Your Profits and Productivity
Noel B. Lorenzana, CPA

potentially eliminate any deductions or credits that cannot be properly verified. They will require documentation to verify the income and expense items in question. From there, they will decide whether to allow or disallow the items on your tax return. Providing a credit card statement to support your deduction is not sufficient. You'll need actual receipts or scanned digital copies (wink) to support your expense deductions on everything.

If the audit determines that you overstated your expenses or understated your income, you'll owe more taxes. You don't have long to pay this additional amount before it accumulates interest. Penalties can also be incurred, especially if they believe you deliberately made errors in an attempt to avoid taxation. The IRS has the power to levy your bank accounts and garnish your wages without a court order. As you probably already realize, an audit is not a pleasant experience.

Remember that letter from the IRS? It may also contain something called a CP2000, which is not an audit. A CP2000 is a deficiency notice letting you know that something is missing or doesn't match up on your return. It's still wise to bring this to your CPA's attention, because it's a chance to correct a mistake or omission on your return.

Best Practices for Staying out of IRS Audit Trouble:

- File your tax returns on time

Modernized Accounting & Technology for the Small Business Owner

- Pay what you owe and when you owe it
- Maintain a proper set of books (i.e. financial accounting records)
- Work with a CPA
- Don't ignore IRS letters
- Save your receipts
- Document all financial activity
- Properly classify workers
- Don't mix business with personal expenses
- Know what's deductible
- Purchase an Audit Protection Plan

Let's look at these individually:

File your tax returns on time. This is one of the easiest items on the list to avoid. The primary cause of late filing is just a lack of preparedness. If you must scramble to find documents or figure out the numbers, you're more likely to be late. Procrastination is the other. Don't wait until the last minute to talk to a tax professional and expect them to have space to fit you into their schedule.

Pay what you owe and when you owe it. Not paying your taxes when due causes several problems. Triggering an audit may be one. Even if not, you might incur a "failure to pay" penalty and owe interest on the unpaid amount. Filing an extension gives you more time to file your tax return, but you still owe the payment due at the original filing deadline.

Increase Your Profits and Productivity
Noel B. Lorenzana, CPA

Maintain a proper set of books. Having your bookkeeping in order is a fundamental practice in business. It also demonstrates to the IRS that you're serious about your business and allows you to verify your expenses and income with accuracy. It also makes it much easier to file your taxes on time, since you won't need an accountant to catch up on months of uncategorized transactions.

Work with a CPA. A Certified Public Accountant with real-world experience and expertise with taxes, accounting, and business assures you the best in service. They can help you stay out of trouble and make it much easier to resolve any issues you may encounter. Obtaining a CPA designation requires passing a rigorous 14-hour examination and obtaining a Bachelor's Degree in Accounting, including 150 credit hours, ethics courses, and regular continuing education.

Don't ignore IRS letters. Believe it or not, IRS problems don't go away by themselves. If you receive an IRS letter, do not ignore it. Failing to respond makes you appear negligent and may lead to additional penalties and interest.

Save your receipts. Properly stored and organized receipts can save you much trouble if you ever must prove your expenses to the IRS. Keep them organized in your files, or better yet, make digital copies for quick access and longevity. As mentioned earlier, you can take a digital picture or scan of a document and save that instead of the physical paper.

Modernized Accounting & Technology for the Small Business Owner

Document all financial activity. File away any records, invoices, receipts, and contracts to verify any financial transactions the IRS might question. You can even use software like Hubdoc or a similar application to digitize the process and make these files searchable.

Properly classify workers. Contrary to popular opinion, IRS guidelines dictate that a worker is an employee or independent contractor. Specific rules dictate the proper classification, and it is not simply a choice by the employer or business owner. Classifying employees as contractors is a common mistake, and an ill-advised way to evade employment taxes. The IRS is vigilant about businesses that may be misclassifying their employees. Employees can report employers after the fact about improper classification, subjecting the business to employment taxes, penalties and interest.

Don't mix business with personal expenses. Combining personal expenses with business expenses is a poor business practice. Not only can it invalidate your legal business structure, it's an opportunity for the IRS to look at not just one, but both your personal and business finances simultaneously. Make sure you have separate business accounts, separate business credit cards, and properly record transactions between your personal and business finances.

Know what's deductible. Never deduct business expenses you're unsure of and assume the IRS will not question it. These items will usually lead to a

Increase Your Profits and Productivity
Noel B. Lorenzana, CPA

deeper investigation of your tax return to make sure that everything else is correct. Allowable business deductions must be ordinary and necessary to your type of business and specifically allowed by the Internal Revenue Code. This is where your CPA can help you again. They know the ins and outs of valid deductions for your business and keep updated on the constant tax code changes.

Purchase an Audit Protection Plan. The truth is anyone is subject to the scrutiny of the IRS for many reasons. With an Audit Protection Plan, you gain the peace of mind of not having to deal with the IRS by yourself. For a small fee, you'll be covered if a notice occurs from the IRS or other state tax authorities. The best part is having a licensed tax professional by your side to defend you.

IRS HOT SPOTS

The following is a quick list of red flags that may alert the IRS. If your business must pass through these "hot spots", some of which may be unavoidable, talk with your tax professional about the best way to proceed.

- Not Reporting All Income
- Home Office Deductions
- Cash Businesses
- Losses for the Self-Employed, Business Owner
- Unusually High Earnings
- Losses From Hobby (ie. IRS classifies your

Modernized Accounting & Technology for the Small Business Owner

business as a hobby)
- High Deductions
- Travel, Meals, and Entertainment
- Business Use of Vehicle
- Foreign Bank Accounts

A quick word on unscrupulous tax preparers… Avoid them. Bottom line. A tax preparer who offers to save you money with questionable practices can get you into trouble with the IRS. It's just not worth it. Do the right thing and work with a reputable professional.

CHAPTER 10

YOUR ACCOUNTANT

So far, we've discussed several tools to leverage technology for your business. We've talked about streamlining your processes and using cloud-based software to work with remote workers and perform work when you are not in the office. With technology, you may not even need an office!

Building a team of outside experts is a great way to utilize knowledge and experience of others without the expense and complications of bringing all these people on as employees. One of the most important additions to this team is your accountant. An experienced, professional accountant, with whom you get along well, can be the difference between business success and business failure. He or she can also be the catalyst for growing your already successful business to the next level.

I say this not as a biased accounting professional, but as someone who has seen how good, timely financial information is crucial to the success of any business. Large corporations have entire departments dedicated to handling this information. On the opposite end of the spectrum, start-ups and many small businesses only connect with their accountant for their yearly tax return. Technology now makes it easy to bring that expert level of financial advising on board. Now you can run with the big boys, even if your business isn't very big.

How do you find the right accountant?

Not all accountants are equally skilled. Let's look at some key differences to consider when looking for an accountant to work with.

Accounting and bookkeeping are different. Bookkeeping is the day-to-day process of entering information into your books and classifying it in the correct categories. It also includes things like bank reconciliations to help ensure that banking transactions have been entered and to detect bank errors. Some accountants offer bookkeeping, and some bookkeepers have degrees in accounting. However, don't expect every bookkeeper to professionally handle your accounting needs, even if they have the word "accounting" in their business name.

Increase Your Profits and Productivity
Noel B. Lorenzana, CPA

Accountants handle a much broader range of financial analysis and advising. They often start with the books compiled by the bookkeeper and go from there, first making sure there are no obvious errors in the information. Your accountant can advise on tax strategy and preparation, cost management, investment, and purchase decisions, and often your personal financial planning too. An experienced accountant can often find the problems in your business or the inefficiencies in your processes.

Finding an accountant who offers bookkeeping services can help streamline the process. Regardless, technology makes it easy to share financial information across your virtual team even if you do the day-to-day bookkeeping yourself. So, how do you find a qualified accountant?

PROFESSIONAL DESIGNATIONS

In the United States, there are several credentials for accountants and tax professionals you should be aware of.

A degreed accountant has received a Bachelor's Degree in Accounting from College or University. They would be well qualified to manage your business bookkeeping and accounting needs. Although, not all accountants are tax preparers. Many avoid taxes, altogether. If you find a degreed accountant to prepare your tax return, make sure they are experienced with taxes and provide the services as a part of their primary business. Be cautious as some may call themselves an accountant when they have no degree in accounting.

One credential that is less commonly known to entrepreneurs is the EA. An Enrolled Agent (EA) is a tax designation awarded by the IRS to those who pass an extensive tax exam. An EA might be a good fit for you if your needs are solely tax related. However, EAs cannot certify financial statements or perform audits or attest work. Accounting and bookkeeping may not be part of an EAs training.

By far, the most widely recognized credential is the Certified Public Accountant or CPA. There is a good reason for this. CPAs have extensive training in a full range of accounting areas and can assist you with tax, strategy, financial management, and just about anything else you need regarding your business finances. Besides extensive education requirements and a rigorous set of exams, CPAs must keep up with continuing education. In addition, most states require the credit equivalent of a master's degree just to sit for the exam.

TRUSTED ADVISOR

Choosing the right accountant is more than accountant vs. bookkeeper, or Enrolled Agent vs. CPA. The real secret to getting the most return on the relationship is finding a professional who truly partners with you throughout the year. By that, I mean they become a part of your team and help you make proactive decisions rather than just taking care

Increase Your Profits and Productivity
Noel B. Lorenzana, CPA

of things at the end of the year. In our complex and competitive business environment, what you need is a trusted advisor.

A trusted business advisor understands your business, has your best interests at heart, and will work with you throughout the year. It's like having someone "on the inside." When there's a tax change or a new piece of technology changes the landscape of business or accounting, your accountant/advisor can give you the highlights right away. Because they understand accounting and take the time to understand your business in depth, they can provide the best possible solutions and strategies to help you navigate your business to success.

CONNECTING YOUR ACCOUNTANT

As you can probably tell, if you want your accountant to be a trusted advisor they must be involved and in touch with you on a regular basis. This allows you to have the information you need to make timely decisions. Fortunately, all the technology we've been talking about makes this possible. Connecting with your accountant has never been easier.

Whatever software you use to handle your accounting, you should be able to grant access to your accountant. Make sure your software's features allow access to those who need it. For instance, different subscription levels of QuickBooks Online accommodate different numbers of users. If you have

Modernized Accounting & Technology for the Small Business Owner

internal users, a remote bookkeeper, and a separate remote accountant, you may need to upgrade to a level that allows more users. You may also be able to grant different levels of access. For example, some may only view reports but not make changes or add transactions to the books. Others may have full access.

Setting your accountant up to view your books is the first step that will allow them to advise you without needing to send or print out statements and deliver them to the accountant each time. It can also make things much easier when it's time to file taxes.

Talk with your accountant to figure out what access they need and why. This will depend on how closely they are advising you and whether they're handling your day-to-day bookkeeping as well. They may need to access documents in a program like Hubdoc or view payable or receivable records in Bill.com.

If managing your books, they will probably need online access to bank accounts with a view only permission. This means they can see statements and account activity but cannot move money or make changes. Safety is crucial but granting the right accesses to an accounting professional can make life easier (as they can pull up information without having to ask you for it) and safer because they can help you monitor what happens in your business.

Increase Your Profits and Productivity
Noel B. Lorenzana, CPA

Remember what I said about a trusted advisor? Having all these tools in place makes that relationship much easier. You can set regular meetings with your accountant to strategize and discuss your business, and he or she can access all your information to prepare for that meeting. It's also easier than ever to meet remotely. Sure, conference calls have been around for years, but an online video conference with the ability to share your screen to analyze the financials is more convenient.

If you've always thought an accountant was just someone you picked out of the phone book to do your taxes each year (maybe like getting a haircut), it's time to update that thinking. Businesses that thrive in a competitive economy do so by understanding the numbers and being proactive. Partnering with a trusted accountant is one of the best steps you can take toward that goal.

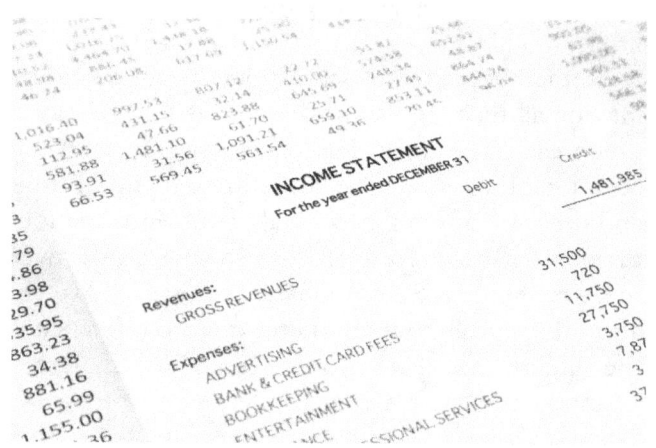

CHAPTER 11

UNDERSTANDING FINANCIAL STATEMENTS

Financial statements are a quantified measure of the health of your business, like blood pressure, cholesterol, heart rate, and other metrics used to track your physical health. You may not be a doctor but understanding what these numbers mean and what yours are will allow you to protect your business' health. Understanding how to read financial statements will allow you to protect your business and know when potential trouble awaits. It also allows you to have more productive conversations with your accountant. This chapter summarizes your basic financial statements and some key indicators to look at when you're reading them.

Increase Your Profits and Productivity
Noel B. Lorenzana, CPA

THE BASICS

Although your accounting software can generate many reports, there are four basic financial statements: the balance sheet, profit-and-loss statement (also called the income statement), statement of shareholders' equity, and the statement of cash flows.

The balance sheet records the assets you own and any debts you owe at a specific point in time. This reveals a company's financial position better than just looking at a bank statement. For instance, a company may have many assets and a large bank balance but also tremendous debt. The "balance" of the two sides will show whether there is any equity in the company.

The income statement shows revenue and expenses over a certain period, usually a month or a year. This information shows whether the company is profitable. A large company with significant reserves may go without profits for a while, but smaller companies must remain profitable to stay in business.

The statement of cash flows shows how much cash has flowed in or out of the business during a period which is often different from the income or expenses because of credit and deferred payments. Cash flow is broken down into cash from operations, investments, and financing.

Finally, the statement of shareholders' equity shows the change in equity from the beginning to the end of a period. Depending on the structure of the company, this could be also be expressed as stockholders', owners', or partners' equity.

These statements fit together like puzzle pieces. Profits or losses from the income statement will be reflected in the balance sheet as net income (or loss), which later is combined with retained earnings. They also impact the cash flow statement. Changes to the balance sheet will end up on the statement of shareholders' equity, which is a part of the balance sheet. Understanding the numbers and communicating them with your accountant will serve you well as a business owner.

Here are critical pieces of information you can find in your financial statements and what they mean for your business:

GROSS PROFIT MARGIN

One of the most important numbers for business owners to know is gross profit or gross profit margin. This is the difference between the cost of an item and the selling price. For example, a product that costs $70 and sells for $100 has a gross profit of $30 or 30 percent. This number is "gross" because it's measured before operating expenses or anything else are factored in. Managing gross profit is crucial because if you want to make a profit, it shows you exactly how much you have available to cover selling expenses, marketing, etc. Insufficient gross profit margin can make it difficult for a business to make a profit, even

Increase Your Profits and Productivity
Noel B. Lorenzana, CPA

with a high sales volume.

One of the simplest uses of the gross profit margin is calculating how many units you must sell to break even or make a certain amount of profit. Since many operating costs are fixed and don't move up and down with selling volume, you can quickly see how many sales you need to cover costs. In our example, you would figure out how many $30 gross profit sales would you need to cover a certain amount of fixed expenses and break even. Alternatively, how many you would need to reach a profit goal, since that $30 goes towards profits once the fixed expenses have been covered.

Many people confuse gross profit margin with markup. This can be especially confusing because markup is vague, and people use it in diverse ways. It is often the percentage of the cost that's added to reach the selling price. Contrast that with gross margin, which is a percentage of the selling price, and you can see how the percentages would differ. Our example is a 30 percent gross profit margin. Measuring markup using the method I've just described would result in an almost 43 percent markup. Be mindful of this when calculating your selling prices.

IT'S A WRITE-OFF!

However, what does that really mean? Not to be confused with "writing off" uncollectible debts, a tax write-off is an expense that is tax deductible and

Modernized Accounting & Technology
for the Small Business Owner

decreases your taxable income by the amount of the expense. It's very important to know what is and what isn't deductible and keeping track of your expenses. Given the recent changes under the new tax reform law, there are some expenses that were previously deductible, which are not any longer.

Thinking of expenses in tax write-offs can also cause a common mistake. We think a deductible write-off is a freebie. "Don't worry about it; it's a write-off!" But remember, this may generate a tax deduction, not a tax credit. That means it doesn't decrease your tax bill directly; it decreases your taxable income. So, the money you save on taxes will be the cost of the deductible expense, multiplied by your marginal tax rate (the rate that applies to the highest portion of your income.) If you have the new corporate tax rate of 21 percent, then your $10,000 expense will decrease your taxable income by $10,000, and your tax savings would be $2100 ($10,000 multiplied by 21%). That means it still costs you $7,900 after taxes. Using this after-tax cost to make decisions will give you a better idea of what you're spending.

There are also expenses that are not deductible. A current example of this is entertainment expenses. They have been a tax write-off for years but were eliminated under the Tax Cuts and Jobs Act. When recording these expenses in your accounting ledger, they must be separated and properly marked as non-deductible. This makes it much easier to sort them out for tax purposes so that you can arrive at an

Increase Your Profits and Productivity
Noel B. Lorenzana, CPA

accurate number for your tax return.

INCOME STATEMENT AND BALANCE SHEET

As I mentioned earlier, the financial statements reflect different aspects of your company's financial health, but they fit together like puzzle pieces. For example, numbers flow from the income statement to the balance sheet and affect each other in different ways. Let's look at some ways these statements interact and how that can affect accurate financials and taxes.

The net profit or net loss number at the bottom of the income statement flows over to the statement of shareholders equity, and impacts retained earnings. This same number is the starting point for the cash from the operations section of the cash flow statement.

Looking at the income statement, business owners are often tempted to skip to the end and search for "the bottom line" i.e., net profit or loss. Though it is tempting to skim past the details, it's there for a reason and focusing only on "the bottom line" gives an incomplete understanding of the accounting process.

Many business owners don't even look at the balance sheet, maybe because that's where debt is recorded, or because it's not well understood. Without a solid understanding of the balance sheet, those income statement figures are likely to be inaccurate. For example, failure to pay attention to the balance sheet can cause you to overlook depreciation expense or to not write down the value of an asset like inventory, which can generate deductible business expenses. This could produce overstated income and would negatively impact your tax bill. Understating your liabilities can also result in overstated income.

These are just a few ways that balance sheet accounts impact the income statement. Business owners who prepare their taxes (or inexperienced tax preparers) often miss these opportunities and end up with a larger tax bill than is owed. These tax strategies can affect how you manage your business throughout the year, so being aware of their impact in advance is essential for decision making.

If this all seems overwhelming, don't worry. Not everyone is a numbers person, and that is likely not why you went into business. The most important thing for business owners is to gain an understanding of the basics and never be afraid to ask questions when you meet with your accountant. Having a professional you trust is key because they are a numbers person and specialize in the important details you may or may not care to think about.

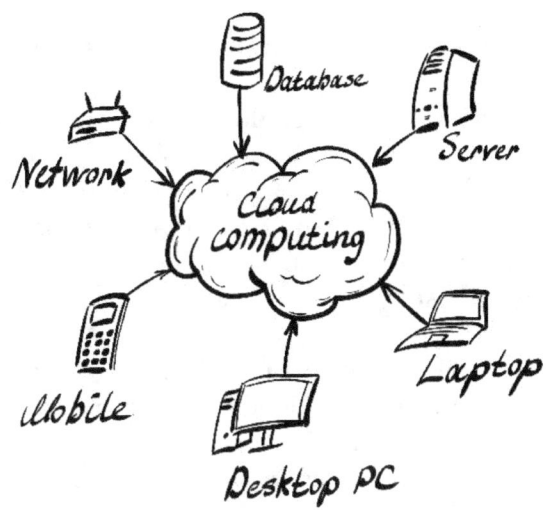

CHAPTER 12

FINAL THOUGHTS

Helped by modern technology, the tools we've talked about will make it much easier to build a team and smoothly run your business. I hope this book has enlightened you to new possibilities, so your business can get to the next level and thrive.

Before we wrap this up, let's do a quick overview of what we've covered. Here are ways to jumpstart your business. You can use some or all of the suggestions, depending on what you're currently doing:

Modernized Accounting & Technology for the Small Business Owner

Your Modernized Accounting System

Whether you're just getting started or have been using a more manual system, consider your options for a cloud-based online accounting system. This is the foundation of the strategies and tools that we've discussed and allows you to leverage technology to get the best results.

QuickBooks Online and Xero are the two strongest companies in cloud-based accounting. Find one that fits your business needs and gives you room to grow. Also, look to work with an accountant who is a certified partner or advisor with your software company of choice.

Digitize Your Documents

Start making the transition to paperless, digital documents so you can easily share information with your team, access files from outside of the office, and attach documents to transactions in your accounting software.

Apps

Look closely at what you do in your business day in and day out. Every business has different needs, and there are great applications out there to make most easier. Depending on your needs, look into apps to store and share documents, organize and pay bills, track time on jobs, track mileage, digitally sign contracts and other documents, manage passwords, etc. Try implementing one at a time, so you have time to learn each one. Trade groups can point you to great apps specific to your industry, and your accountant should be able to help you find others that will make your life easier.

Connect Your Bank

Syncing your accounting software to your bank's secure online banking portal is a great way to verify that your banking financial transactions are properly recorded.

Automate Bills and Invoices

You can minimize the manual labor of bills and invoices by using your online accounting software, applications like Bill.com, and your bank's bill pay services. Setting these up will save you a lot of time and energy each month.

Digital Security

A digital office can be more secure than a paper one, but it requires different safety measures. Use secure passwords and limit access to only those who need it. Use separation of duties to provide checks and balances against abuse of access. Make sure you backup your digital information (don't worry, most of this is done automatically by your software).

Modernized Accounting & Technology for the Small Business Owner

OUTSOURCE

You can use your new tech tools to monitor, share, and communicate with a remote team, allowing you to outsource parts of your operation to specialists outside of your office. Gain efficiency by taking your weaknesses off of your plate and focusing on what you do best.

TAKE A HOLISTIC VIEW

Remember the three major areas where many businesses succeed or fail: sales and marketing, production/business operations, accounting, and taxes. Be aware of all three areas and use the tools and your team to strengthen your weak areas. A great product is no good if you can't sell it. Neither is a great sales process when you can't keep up with production. Tax and accounting strategies make both more valuable as you maximize your after-tax profits, and keep out of tax trouble.

DON'T FEAR THE IRS

It's easy to be afraid of the IRS, which is one of their objectives. Their ability to collect taxes through a wide range of means is intimidating but you only have to follow simple rules and you need not worry about an IRS audit. Keep records of everything, use a strategy that works with the tax code, not one that tries to illegally evade taxes, and work with an accountant with knowledge and experience in dealing with IRS issues.

Increase Your Profits and Productivity
Noel B. Lorenzana, CPA

PARTNER WITH AN ACCOUNTANT

Finally, partner with a great accountant who has your best interests in mind. He or she will be part of your team and should be committed to helping you succeed. Find someone willing to be an advisor throughout the year and not just someone who does the bookkeeping. Discussions can be included in an accountant's monthly pricing or for an additional charge. This will make the decision-making process and strategy on a month-to-month basis much easier and remove the guesswork.

Do you need help to make it all happen?

I hope the information in this book has helped you get started in the right direction. Tools and technology can make a huge difference in the success of a business. But, let's be honest, many business owners are overwhelmed by the thought of making changes and aren't sure how to maximize this whole process.

I'd love to help!

Throughout this book, I've talked about the importance of an accountant as a trusted advisor who goes above and beyond for your business and helps you take a proactive approach towards growth. This is the standard I live by in my practice. I'd love to schedule a consultation with you to help you find the best step to take first.

Modernized Accounting & Technology for the Small Business Owner

Thanks for taking time to read my book. Send me an email to noel@lorenzanatax.com to say hello and let me know your thoughts. If you would like to book a consultation visit noelblorenzana.com/booking.

www.ingramcontent.com/pod-product-compliance
Lightning Source LLC
Chambersburg PA
CBHW071422220526
45469CB00004B/1386